WEYMOUTH
REVISITED

MAUREEN ATTWOOLL
and
COLIN A. POMEROY

DORSET BOOKS

First published in Great Britain in 2004

British Library Cataloguing-in-Publication Data
A CIP record for this title is available from the British Library

ISBN 1 871164 44 3

DORSET BOOKS
Official publisher to Dorset County Council

Halsgrove House
Lower Moor Way
Tiverton, Devon EX16 6SS
Tel: 01884 243242
Fax: 01884 243325
email: sales@halsgrove.com
website: www.halsgrove.com

Printed and bound by CPI, Bath

CONTENTS

ACKNOWLEDGEMENTS

The 300-plus illustrations in this book have been brought together from a number of sources and we are very grateful to all those who contacted us to offer pictures, some very generously contributing precious photographs from their own collections for inclusion in *Weymouth Revisited*. One of the most enjoyable aspects of compiling a book such as this is discovering so many local people willing to share their knowledge of the town and its history with us.

Many of the pictures reproduced are from the comprehensive Illustrations Collection which is part of the Local Studies Collection at Weymouth Library, and we thank the staff there for their assistance and patience as we made our selection.

Others we must thank are David Murdock, Editor of the *Dorset Echo* who gave us permission to use a number of 1950s and 1960s photographs which originally appeared in the newspaper; Andy and Jenny Miller also contributed a number of excellent photographs from this period. Brian Jackson, as ever, provided invaluable help with transport topics as well as supplying and copying illustrations for us. Joe Ward and Colin Caddy, whose cameras miss very little of local history interest, offered us excellent photographs taken in recent years. Geoff Hounsell, lent us some rare views from his postcard collection.

David Attwooll, Michael and Barbara Box, Ian Brooke of Brooke Photographic, Alan Fowler, the late Graham Herbert, Audrey Johnson, Bill Macey, HMS *Osprey* Photographic Section, the late Eric Ricketts, Ted Tranter, Jack West, Richard 'Knocker' White and Cecil and Margaret Woodcock all contributed pictures and/or information.

Our grateful thanks to all who assisted, and of course, to our respective spouses David Attwooll and Binks Pomeroy without whose assistance *Weymouth Revisited* would not have been completed on time – if at all!

INTRODUCTION

Through illustrations which span four centuries, *Weymouth Revisited* takes another look at the changing face of the town and its surrounding villages. Artists began depicting this favourite holiday haunt of royalty when King George III's visits to the seaside in the late 1700s brought Weymouth fame as England's premier health and pleasure resort. In the days before the invention of the camera, paintings and engravings of the seafront, harbour, town and countryside were popular souvenirs which visitors might purchase to take home and display as a reminder of their stay by the sea.

One of the best-known (and now much collected) artists of the early nineteenth century was John William Upham, who taught at St Mary's School, which until the 1980s occupied the site of the present Weymouth Library in Great George Street. Upham depicted Weymouth in a number of paintings and produced eighteen of these as engravings in a series entitled 'Views in and near Weymouth', advertising them for sale in the *Dorset County Chronicle* in July 1825 at 8 shillings each (plain) and 12 shillings each (coloured).

When John Love published a volume of prints by different artists in 1790, he dedicated it to HRH The Duke of Gloucester, younger brother of King George III, in recognition of the Duke's patronage of the resort. It was to the Duke's house, Gloucester Lodge on Weymouth Esplanade, that King George III came in the summer of 1789 to recover from the much misunderstood episode of 'madness' that he had suffered the previous year.

Included too, is the work of William Pye, an artist who depicted Weymouth in the latter half of the nineteenth century and the early years of the twentieth. Pye, who lived at Rodwell, also contributed to the local pictorial guides, and the advertisements contained in them featured very fine engravings of local shop and business premises – many easily recognisable today, once modern street level shopfronts have been by-passed and attention is focused on the façades above them.

By the end of the nineteenth century photography had developed apace. Some of the earliest known photographs of Weymouth were taken by local man William Thompson, who is also recognised as a pioneer of underwater photography. At the close of the Victorian era the town was being very well recorded in photographs, the numbers of which increased dramatically when the craze for collecting picture postcards caught on in the early years of the twentieth century. In the years before World War I postcards could be sent through the post for one halfpenny, half the cost of a letter, and millions of view cards were produced bearing photographs of cities, towns, villages and resorts up and down the country. Although the cost of postage has increased, the holiday tradition of sending a 'Wish you were here' picture postcard to those back at home still continues, although it is now possibly under threat from e-mail and text messaging.

Sometimes a scene changes surprisingly little as the years pass, but often modern developments and many years' tree growth preclude the present-day photographer from capturing a view from the same spot as a previous artist or photographer. Occasionally a more general overview of the site of an old picture has been included if a modern exact match is of little interest.

Weymouth Revisited brings together a selection of views old and new; scenes well-known and less familiar in a collection of pictures which illustrate Weymouth and its environs from 1790 to 2004.

ABBOTSBURY ROAD

The suburb of Westham developed in the latter half of the nineteenth century and its growing population was served by this row of shops at the junction of Abbotsbury Road and Holland Road, seen here in the early 1900s. The business on the corner was Bugler's, a fruit and veg shop, which also offered carriages for hire. One of the firm's vehicles and the entire Bugler family have lined up outside for the photograph.

Apart from shopfronts, little had changed by the 1980s...

...but today the first-floor bay windows, formerly set back within brick arches, have been incorporated into new facades flush with the front of the terrace. The building in the foreground has been extended into Holland Road and is now a doctors' surgery.

The terrace, seen from the opposite direction at the junction of Abbotsbury Road and Newstead Road, in the 1980s.

The single storey corner shop and the property behind it were demolished to make way for 'Marcel Court', a residential and shop development, in 1990.

ALEXANDRA GARDENS

The Alexandra Gardens Theatre of 1924 (left) was still functioning as a theatre when this view was taken in 1960, but the new Pavilion Theatre opened that summer and competition proved too great for both to survive. The Alexandra Gardens Theatre closed in 1963 and the building and gardens around it were converted to Amusements shortly afterwards.

Forty years on, rides and slot machines still tempt holiday visitors but the amusements are now housed in a purpose-built complex in the gardens, a replacement of the old Theatre, which burned down in 1993.

The original two-storey Alexandra Gardens café, shown here in an early 1950s postcard view, has since been replaced by a refreshment kiosk. Around the perimeter of the gardens once stood six thatched shelters dating from the early 1900s, but these were gradually removed in the years following World War II and none now remain. Two of these rustic structures were brick-lined during the war, as can be seen here, and used as air raid shelters.

Right: A building which overlooked the scene long before the Alexandra Gardens existed is still there today, converted now to apartments. This was originally the old 'Bank' of Bank Buildings, later converted to become Voss's Boarding House. Enlarged and refurbished in the 1870s, it became the Marine Hotel, as seen here in the early 1900s, then the Edward Hotel and finally the Hotel Dumonts.

A scene from the gardens in 2004. The refreshment kiosk can be seen in the background.

BINCLEAVES

In the latter part of the twentieth century modern housing requirements brought about the demolition of a number of substantial Victorian and Edwardian properties which dated from an age when families were larger, servants lived in and gardeners were employed to keep rambling grounds under control. Bincleaves House occupied a fine site at the end of Bincleaves Road, overlooking Portland Harbour. Boarded up and due for demolition when this photograph was taken towards the end of 1977, the house made way for an apartment block, Dolphin Court and the houses of Redcliff View.

The grander houses often had a lodge built beside entrance gates and although the gate pillars and drive leading up to Bincleaves House are long gone, its lodge, shown here, still stands.

These apartments now occupy the site of the old house.

BINCOMBE

This very rural and traffic-free scene at Bincombe probably dates from around 1920. Today the village, later used as a 'rat run' by motorists attempting to avoid queues along Dorchester Road, is once again relatively quiet as the turning leading down to Bincombe from Ridgeway Hill is now a 'No Through Road'.

The village street scene today.

Bincombe nestles sleepily below Ridgeway Hill, but for just a few minutes in the 1940s the tiny hamlet found fame when one of the best-known Dorset dialect broadcasters, Ralph Wightman, described the celebration of Christmas in the little country community. A vast audience had tuned in their wireless sets to await King George VI's traditional Christmas Day message, so Wightman's words were heard all over the world.

Holy Trinity Church, Bincombe, has its origins in the twelfth century. In the church-yard are buried two young German soldiers who were shot for desertion in 1801 when they attempted to sail away from Weymouth and their duty of guarding the town during the visits of King George III. They lie in unmarked graves. Around this tragic incident Thomas Hardy based his story of 'The Melancholy Hussar'. This photograph and the previous one date from the 1960s.

Long gone now, the cottage on the right-hand side of this pair is believed to have housed Bincombe's first village school.

Local artist Will Pye's etching is entitled 'Old Cottages at Bincombe', and depicts a now-demolished row of cottages near the church, the earliest of which dated from the Tudor period.

Bincombe Tunnel is Dorset's longest railway tunnel and takes the railway line through Ridgeway for 817 yards. Unlike the one in this pre-electrification photograph, today a goods train would be most unusual.

BOWLEAZE COVE

Cows have ambled down to the water's edge in this very rural 1920s' view of Bowleaze Cove, where only a few beach huts and a handful of deckchairs suggest a holiday scene.

The striking art deco 'Riviera Hotel' went up at Bowleaze in the late 1930s – a building project which was to bankrupt its first owner. Used as a wartime home for disabled evacuee children, the Riviera was later bought by Sir Fred Pontin and became part of his holiday camp empire. Since this 1938 photograph was taken, chalets have been added at first floor level along its entire length. The hotel's modernist design and the innovative use of concrete in its construction have in recent years led to Grade II Listed Building status being conferred on the Riviera, which is currently owned by Hollybush Hotels.

The great boom in caravan holidays began after World War II, and this early 1950s' postcard shows 'Waterside Camp' at Bowleaze, one of several which sprang up in the Preston area.

Waterside Camp's entrance is still in the same place, but the camp, with all its modern facilities, bears little resemblance to the very basic holiday park of fifty years ago.

BROADWEY

Jubilee Terrace still stands on Dorchester Road at Broadwey and its present inhabitants would no doubt prefer the horse-drawn delivery vehicles and bicycles of an earlier age passing close to their front doors. Opposite the cottages stood Devenish's 'Railway Inn'.

Today's view: The inn, also known as the Railway Hotel and, later as the Railway Station Hotel, has been converted to housing.

St Nicholas Church, Broadwey is seen here in an 1825 engraving by John William Upham. Upham was well-known for his local views and this was one of a set of eighteen engravings which were available either as black-and-white or hand-coloured versions (the origin of the expression 'penny plain: twopence coloured' was derived from the sale of prints, but Upham's pictures, now much sought after, were a good deal more expensive than this even then!).

Broadwey Church is of ancient foundation and although many architectural details from its early history remain, the church was much rebuilt and extended throughout the nineteenth century.

Further extensions to the front of the building in the early years of the twentieth century have greatly altered the Broadwey Church of Upham's view.

This cottage in Watery Lane, photographed in the 1920s, was not far from the railway bridge which carried the line to Abbotsbury. It was once known as 'Shepherd's Cottage' and was replaced later in the twentieth century by a bungalow, but in 2004 this has also been demolished and a house now stands on the site.

Upwey and Broadwey Railway Station, with a Merchant Navy class engine heading a five coach passenger service on the down line heading for Weymouth in the 1960s. This station, in the days when the Abbotsbury Railway (1885-1952) branched off here, was formerly known as Upwey Junction.

Candle auctions, sometimes held in agricultural communities for the sale or letting of land, were not uncommon in earlier centuries and survived into the twentieth. This one was held at Broadwey's village school in around 1920. The most usual form of selling by this method was for bids to be made as a candle (quite a short one!) slowly burned down, the successful bid being the last one made before the flame died. This particular auction was to let a meadow at Nottington, the land having originally been left by William Gould as a charitable gift in the seventeenth century. The money obtained from the letting was used to alleviate the distress of the poor in the parish.

Broadwey once had a second railway station – known as Upwey – on the Abbotsbury branch, this name being chosen to avoid confusion with Broadway in Worcestershire. It was renamed Upwey Goods after the branch line's closure in 1952 and served for a few more years, eventually closing in 1961. Later that decade, as we see here, in a sea of mud, the area was developed as a business venture, which today still retains the station building.

BURDON HOTEL

Victoria Terrace & Burdon Hotel
WEYMOUTH

On Weymouth Esplanade, in the centre of Victoria Terrace, stands the former Burdon Hotel, completed in the mid-1850s. Little engravings, such as this one, were sold as holiday souvenirs in the days before picture postcards were introduced.

Just why the name Burdon was chosen is unclear. One of the town's leading citizens in the nineteenth century was one William Wharton Burden, but his surname is spelt differently. In this 1880s' guidebook illustration the hotel is advertised as the 'Imperial Burdon Hotel'.

Since 1971 the former 'Burdon' has been known as the Hotel Prince Regent. Its façade has altered very little in 150 years.

BUXTON ROAD

This scene from around 1900 is almost impossible to recreate today. Houses on Buxton Road have since filled the site on the right hand side of the picture, and over a period of one hundred years, trees have grown up all around the route of the defunct Weymouth and Portland Railway. Bereft of its lines and sleepers, this is now the 'Rodwell Trail'. The railway cutting can just be recognised, dipping away on the left hand side of the photograph. The brick pillar visible stands at the start of Buxton Road Bridge which takes the road over the railway, close to Clearmount Road. The house in the centre of the picture is 'Glenthorn' and it, and the more distant properties, are in Old Castle Road.

These houses, dating from the early 1900s, fill the site shown on the right in the previous photograph.

Just around the corner, in Longfield Road, lived local artist William Pye. This is his own sketch of his house, 'Dunmore', in 1894. Today it stands little altered, apart from the replacement of railings along the frontage by a hedge. Will Pye was a noted landscape artist and he also produced etchings of scenes in and around Weymouth, some of which are reproduced in this book. Born in Lancashire in 1853, he lived in Weymouth for more than fifty years and died here in 1934.

CHICKERELL ROAD

A typical 'corner shop' in pre-supermarket days stood at the junction of Chickerell Road and Prince of Wales Road and was in the ownership of one family for almost a century, first as Higgins Stores, and later as Woodcock & Son. It is seen here in the period of the 1914-18 War.

An earlier twentieth century view, taken from the Weymouth and Portland Railway line bridge, shows that the shop (foreground, left) also housed Pyehill Post Office.

Shortly prior to decimalization, here we see the proprietors Cecil and Margaret Woodcock outside the thriving corner shop...

...which, after several changes of ownership, now stands empty and boarded-up.

Currently the headquarters of the local branch of the Loyal Order of Moose, the former Old Borough Arms public house at 137 Chickerell Road has changed little in outward appearance since this photograph was taken some one hundred years ago.

This row of six houses stands almost opposite Hardy Avenue on Chickerell Road and in the mid 1920s enjoyed a quite rural setting.

Today Chickerell Road has almost doubled in width and houses stretch along its length on both sides. Apart from minor changes, the houses in the older picture still look much as they did eighty years ago.

CHICKERELL VILLAGE

The Lugger Inn is one of half-a-dozen pubs that were once within Chickerell's boundaries. An ancient hostelry, it also occupied adjacent thatched cottages and these were damaged by fire in February 1912. This photograph was taken the following day with the burnt-out section just visible in the background. 'The Lugger', commented the local press in its account of the blaze, 'stands in Cow-lane, or rather, we should say, to give the locality its more recent and aristocratic title, West street...'

The Lugger closed in 1996 but in 2003 it re-opened for business again. Additions to the building have completely changed its appearance, but the tall chimney can be picked out in both photographs.

Another of Chickerell's pubs was once housed in these cottages at Bakehouse Corner, close to where the road off Garston Hill leads into the village. The 'Red Lion' occupied the thatched cottage (now demolished) in the background. Elm Cottage, next to it, still stands. The cottages on the left of the picture have since been completely rebuilt. The photograph probably dates from the 1920s.

Numbers 490-494 Chickerell Road, built in 1952, now fill the site of the cottages on the left-hand side of the old picture, but Elm Cottage can be found in both views. Remnants of an oven from the old bakery at 'Bakehouse Corner' still exist here.

Chickerell's Putton Lane Brickworks flourished from around the middle of the nineteenth century until its closure in 1965, initially producing bricks and, later, tiles and chimneypots. The tall chimneys are seen here shortly before their demolition in October, 1980. Today, Bennett's tranquil and beautifully landscaped water gardens occupy this former industrial site.

Crook Hill Brickworks were sited just off the main road (B3157) at Chickerell and produced a wide variety of wares such as pipes, chimneys and pots as well as the very hard red 'Chickerell bricks'. In this snowy scene from the winter of 1962-63 'Brickyard Terrace', originally workers' cottages, can be seen in the background. The brickworks were in operation from the mid nineteenth century until closure in 1969, although the chimneys remained until 1994. Weymouth and Portland Borough Council depot now occupies the site. At one time Crook Hill Brickworks was owned by the Crickmay family, architects of scores of buildings in and around Weymouth.

COMMERCIAL ROAD

A fine panoramic photograph from the early 1950s focuses on the once- thriving commercial and industrial waterfront area along Commercial Road. Marine engineers Cosens and Company's workshops were situated here – the company's paddle steamer *Embassy* can be seen tied up alongside.

Today the Inner Harbour has been converted to a Marina and its waters are crowded with pleasure craft. Very few of the original buildings along the length of Commercial Road survive and apartment blocks (shown here), shops and car parks have replaced them.

This part of Commercial Road, known as Ferrys Corner, is easily recognisable in the first view by the distinctive chimneys of the building in the centre of this picture, taken before the corner was widened. The little structure behind the billboards has since been replaced by harbourside flats. Probably dating from the 1930s, the posters display some well-known names – Boots, Timothy Whites, Shell, Oxo, Ovaltine and Bovril.

Almost all the buildings shown on this 1970s photograph of Commercial Road disappeared in the 1980s when the area was cleared for redevelopment. Webb Major's premises are shown in the centre of the picture; the white building in the background was Kennedy's builders' merchants, which stood on the corner of Lower Bond Street. Beyond it was the tall Jubilee Hall (later the Gaumont Cinema), which was also demolished.

A total change of scene in 2004, with the remaining railway lines of the defunct Weymouth Harbour Tramway providing the only recognisable link.

Often a problem as the trains approached on the town's unique 'railway through the streets' were vehicles left too close to, or even on, the line. This car's owner was no doubt surprised to find his car had been 'spirited away' to a different parking spot when he returned to collect it. The distinctive chimneys in the background belong to the Arts Centre, sole survivor today of the buildings shown here.

CROWN HOTEL

This sketch, the only known picture of the first 'Crown Inn', is based on one made by an eighteenth century Swiss artist, Samuel Hieronymous Grimm, who was commissioned to make a series of Dorset drawings. More than 200 of them are now in the British Museum, and all were drawn in 1790. That year, according to contemporary guidebooks, the Bath and Bristol stagecoach delivered its passengers to the hostelry on Mondays, Wednesdays and Fridays. Those making the return journey on Tuesdays, Thursdays and Saturdays had to be up and about early as the coach left the Crown at 5 a.m.

In the nineteenth century, the Crown Hotel replaced the old Crown Inn on the same site at the lower end of St Thomas Street.

Still clearly recognisable, but almost 'encapsulated' by tall red-brick extensions of the twentieth century, the Crown Hotel of the previous picture is in the centre of this modern photograph. The enlargement of the hotel came in the late 1920s, at the same time as the present Town Bridge was built.

CUSTOM HOUSE QUAY

Sadly now remembered for its rather dilapidated condition in the 1950s, as seen here, the once rather fine early-nineteenth century 'Red Warehouse' stood on the corner of Lower St Mary Street and Custom House Quay.

A scene from October 1958, and demolition was obviously about to begin as the pavement around the building has been fenced off. Some of local salvage expert and general shipping contractor Louis Basso's vessels are moored in the foreground.

The warehouse was pulled down at the end of 1958 and eventually the resulting ugly gap in the harbourside buildings was filled by this extension to the Ship Inn.

DONKEYS

Seaside donkey rides at Weymouth date back to Victorian times, with one family, the Downtons, having provided children's rides on these patient creatures from that time until 2000, when John Downton and his donkeys retired.

A proper observance of the lunch break!

ESPLANADE

Posing in attitudes of studied nonchalance, everyone on the Esplanade in this 1870s' photograph was very aware that they were in the frame. Many of the seafront buildings are still easily recognisable today, but take a look at the little building with the white awning on the corner of Bond Street. Then it was occupied by a drapery business...

... but in the 1880s the site of the draper's shop was filled with one of Weymouth's most picturesque buildings – a pink and white striped flight of fancy which was built as Stuckey's Bank. Stuckey's was later taken over by the Westminster Bank which then merged with National Provincial, and moved into St Thomas Street, where it is now known as the NatWest Bank.

Today this rather splendid former bank building houses public conveniences!

A nostalgic view of the northern end of the seafront in the 1930s. In 1920 there had been proposals to move the Edwardian Bandstand when a site for Weymouth War Memorial was under consideration, but it remained here until 1939 when it was replaced by the Pier Bandstand which, in turn, was partially removed in 1986.

A 1954 Esplanade view shows the 1930s' bus shelter that had been erected directly in front of Weymouth's best-known monument, the statue of King George III. The following year the shelter was demolished when the road system here was re-designed and the King's Statue traffic island constructed.

The Pier Bandstand: the seaward section was removed in 1986, and only the land-based section on the Esplanade remains today. Weymouth War Memorial stands nearby – it was dedicated on 6 November 1921.

At the opposite end of the Esplanade was the Skee Ball pavilion, housing a rather hazardous type of bowling game that was at the height of its popularity in the Twenties. The little structure was taken down in the late 1940s.

'What shall we do now?' They have donned plastic macs and headscarves, but these holidaymakers still seem uncertain where to go on a rainy day at the seaside in the 1950s.

John Upham's view of 1802 depicts even more severe weather conditions as waves batter the Esplanade. The building in the centre background is the 'Bank' which gave its name to Bank Buildings. The infill in front of the Bank, which would provide the ground on which Devonshire and Pulteney Buildings and the Alexandra Gardens stand, was not commenced until several years later.

This engraving shows how the Esplanade followed a much straighter line before the infilling of 1805 took the promenade out in a curve at its southern end. The perspective and a hint of artistic licence suggest a rather distant view of the Esplanade buildings, but there had not been a great deal of development along the seafront when it was drawn in 1790. The third building from the left is the old Theatre Royal and the terrace beyond it is York Buildings (at the back of M&S today). The distant buildings represent Gloucester Row.

The 'Royal' was the first building on what was to become Weymouth Esplanade's Gloucester Row, and it was the resort's first purpose-built high-class hotel. Originally more modestly known in the 1770s as Stacie's Hotel, after its first proprietor, it took the name 'Royal Hotel' when the royal family's residence, Gloucester Lodge, was built next door and King George III and his entourage began their regular summer visits to Weymouth. Demolished in 1891, the elegant first Royal Hotel stood on the same site as today's Victorian hotel of the same name.

Unfortunately, it transpired that although the Victorians had pulled down the Georgian Royal Hotel in 1891 because it was too small and too plain for their liking, no-one had sufficient funds immediately available to replace it. Thus the sizeable gap shown here in the line of Esplanade buildings remained unfilled for several years. Eventually, in 1897, work commenced on the present 'Royal', which opened in 1899.

The Royal Hotel of 1899, its elaborate façade providing a complete contrast to the simple elegance of the earlier Esplanade houses.

The large hotels provided transport to carry guests and luggage from the railway station to their accommodation. This is the Royal's coach in the early years of the twentieth century.

FERRYBRIDGE

A journey to Portland until well into the nineteenth century entailed a boat ride across the waters of the Fleet at Smallmouth, as there was no 'Ferrybridge' until 1839. This is John Upham's view of the ferry in 1807, showing the cottages that afforded shelter for passengers waiting on the Wyke shore.

An earlier engraving published by John Love in 1790 looks towards Wyke Regis, with the tower of All Saints' Church in the background. The ferry was tethered and the ferryman pulled the boat and its passengers across on a rope. Carriages and those on horseback were able to ford across at low water.

The destruction of the ferry during a storm of hurricane force in November 1824, known forever afterwards as the 'Great Gale', led to renewed demands for a bridge to the Island. Progress was slow and it was not until 1839 that the first road bridge, a wooden structure, opened to traffic. By the time this drawing was made, a second timber bridge had been constructed in the 1860s to take the Weymouth and Portland Railway across Smallmouth.

Both wooden road and rail bridges were later replaced by steel structures. The steel rail bridge was removed in 1971, six years after the closure of the railway. The road bridge, shown here, dated from the 1890s. When it began to show severe signs of wear in the late 1970s the decision was taken to cut a new channel and build a new bridge a little closer to Portland. This old bridge was then demolished, the stretch of water it crossed having been infilled.

A close-up of the 1890s' road bridge, which was designed by eminent Victorian engineer John Coode. The car crashing spectacularly through its railings in 1964 was being driven by a stunt man for a scene in the sci-fi feature film 'The Damned'.

Today's Ferrybridge, completed in 1984.

FIRE!

A christening on Weymouth seafront as Miss Hilda Templeman, the Mayor's daughter, names the town's new steam fire engine *The Gem of Weymouth* in September, 1899. The Volunteer Fire Brigade had been formed two years earlier and its equipment prior to this had consisted of just two hose carts and a 30-foot ladder. Messrs Merryweather and Sons patent *Gem* engines were capable of delivering 400 gallons of water per minute. The fire engine was housed then in rather cramped conditions in an ancient building on the corner of St Edmund Street and Maiden Street (since converted to a public convenience).

The badge of the old Weymouth Fire Brigade. It had remained a volunteer brigade until 1938, when local authorities were required to provide a fire-fighting service. After wartime nationalisation it became part of the Dorset Fire Brigade in 1948.

The *Gem* was called out to a serious fire at Sutton Poyntz in April, 1908 which destroyed cottages, farm buildings and some livestock. The blaze engulfed a row of buildings, mostly thatched, but firemen managed to confine the fire to one side of the street.

3 March, 1927, and the Gloucester Hotel is ablaze; a fire which destroyed the interior of the building, although the Georgian facade of the former royal residence was saved.

The art deco architectural design of the Amusements at No 3 Gloucester Row is startlingly different from its Georgian neighbours in the terrace, and the reason for its re-building in 1935 is a tragic one. The ground floor of the original No 3 was occupied by Dan Guy's garage business, above which was the family home. At around midnight on 14 November 1934 fire broke out, and although several people escaped from the burning building, an elderly lady who was visiting died in the blaze and Mr Guy died from injuries he received when he fell from a window.

13 April, 1954 is a date recalled by many locals who watched as black smoke drifted over the town from the fire which destroyed the Ritz Theatre. The largely wooden structure (formerly The Pavilion Theatre) had stood at the pier entrance since 1908.

13 September 1993 saw another seafront theatre go up in smoke – the former Alexandra Gardens Theatre building, which by then had housed an amusement arcade for almost thirty years. A replacement amusements complex has since been built on the site.

Major fires are, thankfully, a rare occurrence in the town centre. The destruction of Maiden Street Methodist Church, seen here ablaze on the morning of 17 January 2002 was a huge blow for its congregation, especially as the church had recently undergone extensive renovation. It was also a great loss to the townscape, as the Victorian building provided an attractive focal point at the end of St Edmund Street. It is now an empty, roofless shell.

The present Weymouth Fire Station, opened in 1939.

Seen here in front of their current JDC Sabre 'first-away' vehicle are members of the 'White Watch' fire crew in March 2004. From left, Firefighters Stuart Rowland, Nick Rodway, Leading Firefighter Martin Ryan, Firefighter Henry Asman and Sub Officer Alan Briggs.

FLEET

Fleet abounds with tales of smugglers and shipwrecks, and its place in literature was firmly established by John Meade Falkner's classic adventure story *Moonfleet*, first published in 1898, reprinted many times since then and also dramatised for television in recent years. The smuggling tale takes its title from the Mohun family, prominent in the village for generations. It is thought that Fleet House, shown here in an engraving of around 1860, has its origins in the seventeenth century when it was built for Maximilian Mohun.

Fleet House today is the popular Moonfleet Hotel, with its wonderful views of Chesil Beach and The Fleet.

When the November 1824 'Great Gale' struck the local area there was great destruction and loss of life at Portland as the sea rose over Chesil Beach and engulfed houses at Chiswell. At Weymouth, where boats floated down the town's main streets, huge seas damaged the Esplanade and the harbour piers. At Fleet cottages were demolished and, close to the beach, the little parish church was almost completely washed away. Eric Ricketts painting recreates the scene before the gale destroyed Fleet Church.

All that is left of the original Fleet Church. What remained was restored and the little building at this now-peaceful spot contains memorials to the Mohun family.

When the new Holy Trinity Church was built at Fleet, it was on a site well out of reach of the seas of the West Bay.

GAUMONT CINEMA

Probably best remembered as the Gaumont, the cinema in St Thomas Street later became the Odeon, then the New Invicta, prior to its final use as a bingo venue. The building had started life in 1887 as the Jubilee Hall and it was revamped in 1926, reopening as The Regent Theatre and Dance Hall. In the 1950s, a lack of industrial workshops in the town led to the former Dance Hall's occupancy by a radio factory for a few years before the building, with its entrance in Mulberry Terrace, reverted to leisure use as a nightclub. The Cinema and Dance Hall buildings, by now a bingo hall and night club, were demolished in the late 1980s in anticipation of a new shopping centre – which was not actually completed until 2000. Patrons of the cinema entered through these doors in St Thomas Street, then made their way via a long corridor to the main auditorium, not visible in this picture.

A view of the interior of the Gaumont Cinema in 1968, shortly after it had been restored to its 1920s' art deco glory. In its Regent days it had been advertised as 'The wonder house of the west', with 900 seats in the stalls and a further 400 in the balcony.

The Jubilee Hall dominates this photograph, taken after the start of demolitions along Commercial Road in the 1980s. Prior to its conversion as the Regent in 1926, the Hall had hosted entertainments as diverse as circuses and balls as well as showing early moving pictures. Its adjacent 'Arcadia' was later to become the Dance Hall, and the floors of both buildings were put to daytime use as rinks during the roller skating craze of the early 1900s.

When the old Gaumont cinema entrance and adjacent shops in St Thomas Street were demolished, the fine facade of the 'Old Rectory' previously hidden behind them could be seen once more. (See a glimpse of it in the first photograph.) After much restoration work this building, set back from its neighbours, now adds a touch of early-nineteenth century elegance to the street scene.

THE
VICTORIA JUBILEE HALL,
WEYMOUTH.

(Erected by the Weymouth and Melcombe Regis Baths, Public Entertainment and Recreation Company, Limited.)
Chairman, Sir Richard Howard; Secretary, Mr. Henry Nangle.

THE PROMENADE HALL.

THE PUBLIC RECREATION BUILDINGS are intended for Concerts, Balls, Meetings, and general Recreation purposes; library and reading-room, gymnasium, and billiard-rooms will also be provided. The large hall, 128 ft. long by 97 ft. wide, containing 12,400 superficial feet of floor space, is divided into a wide and lofty nave 56 ft. high, and aisles on either side. When arranged for a concert or other entertainment, it will accommodate upwards of 3,000 persons in seats, allowing ample room for passages, etc.; or, if required for a large assembly, will hold between 6,000 and 7,000. A high clerestory gives good light and ventilation, and additional light is also obtained from the roof. The site is a convenient and sheltered one in the centre of the town, in a main street, and has no less than five good wide entrances and exits. Ample retiring-rooms and cloak-rooms are also provided, and a large stage, with green-rooms adjacent for performers. Public Baths are to be added, comprising a plunge or swimming-bath, 83 ft. in length by 38 ft. wide, containing 100,000 gallons of water. The swimming-bath is to be 35 ft. high, and have a gallery all round, so that in case of diving or swimming matches there may be ample room for the public to witness the sport. Hot and cold, medical, galvanic, and electric private baths will also be provided, divided into first and second class, for both ladies and gentlemen. The architects are Messrs. Crickmay and Son, of 17, Parliament Street, Westminster, and of Weymouth; and the contractors, Messrs. Joseph Bull, Sons, and Co., of Southampton.

This advertisement features an artist's impression of the Jubilee Hall's interior before it was completed, and it may never have been finished to this elegant standard. The claims for its proposed facilities were rather exaggerated and a promised swimming pool never materialised. It was a gigantic structure and local guidebooks of the period claim that it was able to accommodate 3000 people seated, or 6000-7000 standing. It proved initially to be something of a white elephant and there were complaints about the quality of the acoustics in the hall.

GOVERNOR'S LANE

Any last traces of the town's mediaeval Dominican Friary were lost when all these buildings on the north side of Governor's Lane were demolished in the early 1960s. This old doorway may have been part of the once extensive site occupied by the 'Black Friars' of Melcombe.

The cleared site provided the town with its East Street car park. This scene looks towards the site of the old doorway, beyond the line of cars.

Steward's Court, a little blind alley off Governor's Lane, was included in the demolitions. The 'Governor' of the lane's name was seventeenth-century Parliamentarian Governor of Melcombe Regis, Colonel William Sydenham, who held out against Royalist forces on the other side of the harbour during English Civil War fighting.

HARBOUR

In the late 1950s, their go-kart was forgotten and these lads watched in awe as the cross-channel passenger steamer *St Helier*, originally built for the GWR in 1925, manoeuvred in the Cove. This photograph was taken not long before the end of her life, for the *St Helier* went to the breaker's yard at the end of 1960.

The *St Helier's* sister ship *St Julien*, also built in 1925, departed from Weymouth for the last time in April 1961, destined for Holland and eventual dismantling in 1970. Both vessels and their crews had served with distinction during World War II.

The shipping division of GWR became British Rail Ferries, which in turn was renamed Sealink. This very unusual view shows five Sealink Channel Islands and cross-channel ferries moored in Weymouth Harbour on 3 February 1976. They are, from left, *Caesarea*, *Sarnia*, *Earl Godwin*, *Maid of Kent* and *Caledonian Princess*. Sealink severed its connection with the port in 1987, and since then Condor hydrofoils have carried passengers and vehicles on the service out of Weymouth.

Today's passengers visiting Guernsey, Jersey and St Malo embark on one of Condor's giant Wavepiercer craft for their Channel crossing, such as the *Elanora* seen here.

Two cargo vessels well-known in Weymouth Harbour and originally GWR ships; the *Roebuck* is shown here at the cargo stage...

...and the *Sambur* is on the opposite side of Weymouth Harbour. Before the loss of the tomato contract in 1964, both ships carried many thousands of tons of tomatoes into the port from the Channel Islands in post-war years. These photographs date from the early 1960s.

Grain cargoes were offloaded directly into John Deheer's warehouse via this hopper and conveyor on Custom House Quay. The photograph was taken around 1960. Deheer's closed in 1965 and today the warehouse has been imaginatively converted to the 'Deep Sea Adventure', a popular harbourside tourist attraction.

A photograph taken in the days when pleasure steamers were a familiar sight in the harbour shows two of Cosens and Company's paddle steamer fleet, *Embassy* and *Consul*. It was probably taken in the 1960s, when the era of the excursion steamers was drawing to a close. *Embassy*, the last to leave the port, sailed for the breaker's yard in May, 1967, ending Cosens' 119 year history as excursion steamer operators in Weymouth.

A delightful view of the quay-side in the 1890s – one of Will Pye's evocative etchings.

Out in the Bay, a party of visiting schoolchildren enjoy a trip on the *Weymouth Belle*. The pleasure boat operated here from 1967 until the mid 1970s.

A quite different type of craft operates on Radipole Lake where the 'swan pedaloes' join the real swans on their territory above Westham Bridge. The construction of a new road along the Westham shore in the 1980s has completely changed the scene on the opposite side of the water where the model railway once ran.

JUBILEE CLOCK

The small platform on which the Jubilee Clock stands was originally surrounded by the sand and pebbles of the beach, but Esplanade widening in the 1920s provided not only a broader walkway seaward of the clock, but also formed a barrier to prevent shingle moving southwards onto the sands. This project to extend the Esplanade also provided employment for some of the many local men who returned from the fighting of World War I to find they had no jobs to come home to.

Snow in Weymouth is an unusual sight and this scene at the Jubilee Clock is reminder of the severe winter of 1962-63.

Today's view of the clock is interrupted by the entrance to Weymouth's seafront subway, a 1980s' addition to the Esplanade that takes pedestrians beneath the busy road junction, but does not, as many hoped it would, provide access to the beach.

KING'S STATUE

The King's Statue and the Jubilee Clock are probably Weymouth's best known landmarks. The statue has been a popular assembly point for vehicles since it was erected in 1809-10. Here in the 1920s, when the area in front of the statue was still a vast open space, the horse-drawn carriages and motor charabancs are out in force.

That open space seemed to decrease each year as road traffic grew heavier and by the 1950s vehicles frequently became gridlocked around the monument. The solution was the construction of a large roundabout at the Statue, and since 1955 King George III has looked down on lawns and flowerbeds.

Charmbury, the tobacconist and confectioner, occupied the round house behind the King's Statue in the early years of the twentieth century. Not many pedestrians would risk standing at this spot in the roadway for a chat today. The house shown on the right, No. 18 Royal Terrace, has gone now – it was demolished in 1929 in order to widen the entrance to Westham Road.

LANEHOUSE

Standing, until it burned down in June 1923, on the agricultural land between Wyke Road and Chickerell Road was the thatched farmhouse of Francis Farm. It was completely destroyed and its site is now open land, a short walk from the Cockles Lane footpath which branches off Lanehouse Rocks Road.

No trace of the old farmhouse remains today on the old farmlands of Markham and Little Francis.

LANGTON HERRING

Langton Herring Coastguards have assembled in front of their boathouse on Chesil Beach in the early years of the twentieth century. The boat is a lerret, a sturdy, clinker-built craft specially designed (both fore and aft ends being pointed) for ease of hauling up and down the steep shingle of the beach.

The boathouse in the early 1990s, with the Coastguards of that decade lined up almost exactly as their predecessors of some eighty years before. Today Langton Herring is included in a larger coastguard district and the boathouse on Chesil Beach is now in private ownership. The boat shown here is a trow, the traditional flat-bottomed craft used for crossing the Fleet water.

Will Pye's etching of a Portland lerret appeared in a collection of twelve plates of local views (he added an extra thirteenth plate, of his own house at Rodwell, as an afterthought), which he published for sale in book form in the 1890s.

In the days when picture postcards were often produced to commemorate family occasions, most of the village of Langton Herring has turned out to celebrate a birthday. The group has assembled in what was then a farmyard and they stand at the entrance to Rose's Lane, once a farm track but now a road leading out of the village.

The cottages shown in this photograph and the previous one were once the homes of local fishermen but, now updated, are desirable properties in this attractive village location close to Chesil Beach.

LIBRARY

Weymouth was slow to implement the public library legislation of the nineteenth century and its first public library did not open until 1944, occupying the premises shown here in the Southern Electricity showrooms (known as Electric House) in Westham Road, left vacant during the austere wartime years as there were no electrical goods available for display or sale.

Eventually, after well over forty years in temporary premises, Weymouth Library moved into this new building in the town centre. It stands in Great George Street, on the site formerly occupied by one of the Weymouth's oldest infant and junior schools, St Marys, which closed in 1982. Weymouth Library was opened on 8 November 1990 by HRH Princess Anne.

After the war, the library moved to its second home, another 'temporary' building, this time a post-war prefab at the end of Westwey Road. It was enlarged by the addition of a nearby wartime decontamination centre (which became the Children's Library) and the two separate buildings were 'bridged' in the 1960s by the addition of a new Reference Library (on the right of the photograph).

MONUMENTS AND MEMORIALS

Two statues of Sir Henry Edwards, Victorian benefactor of the town, were once on view in Weymouth. This one can still be seen on the Esplanade, close to the Alexandra Gardens.

This is Edwardsville, Rodwell Avenue, built by Sir Henry Edwards in 1896. It was one of the former MP's many charitable gifts to the town.

At the bottom of Boot Hill, this plaque records the generosity of John Cree, an Osmington man, who paid for road widening here in 1851. Formerly set in a high wall which has since been demolished, the plaque is now sited outside Netherton House.

This second statue of Sir Henry Edwards once stood in the gardens fronting Edwardsville, homes built for the elderly in Rodwell Avenue. Its plinth remains but the statue is no longer on view there.

From 1901 to 1922 Upwey's benefactor was the village's rector, the Reverend Canon William Gildea, who paid for the road to be widened in Elwell Street. This plaque, erected in October 1917, acknowledges his generosity.

The 'Great Gale' of 23 November 1824, which caused devastation all along the south coast, destroyed much of Weymouth's Esplanade and uprooted many of these little stones which, linked by chains, once separated the walkway from the road. This stone records the awful storm, and it is now set in the wall of a raised flowerbed at the southern end of the promenade.

Once mounted on the walls of Weymouth Lifeboat House, these panels record the rescues carried out since the first lifeboat, the *Agnes Harriet* arrived on station in 1869. The boards, too numerous now to display, are currently in the care of Weymouth Museum.

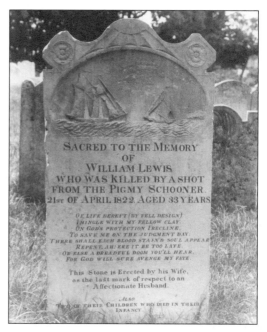

At Wyke a gravestone in All Saints' church-yard declares the innocence of William Lewis. Suspected of smuggling, he was killed in 1822 by a shot 'wantonly and maliciously fired' from a naval schooner.

The delightful thatched bus shelter at Osmington was erected in memory of Lt David Parry-Jones of the Rifle Brigade, killed in action in France on 3 August 1944, and whose parents lived locally. He lies at rest, with 4143 others, at the Commonwealth War Graves Commission Cemetery at Bayeux.

Osmington also has a memorial from World War I, this one to Brigadier General Gordon Strachy Shephard, DSO MC, of the Royal Flying Corps whose aircraft crashed as he was coming in to land at Auchel, in the Nord Pas de Calais on 19 January 1918. He was aged just thirty-two, the youngest officer to hold such a rank in the British Army. The inscribed propeller was erected in the grounds of Shortlake House, his uncle's family home, which is now within the children's holiday activity centre that occupies the site.

NEWSTEAD ROAD

In this 1938 photograph the Odeon Cinema has taken the opportunity to advertise its latest film attraction to motorists held up by roadworks in progress. Properties in the background still stand: today a single-storey blacksmith's and a hair salon, but German bombs destroyed the cottages in World War II. They were replaced by the present bungalows in the late 1960s.

There was more rebuilding on the other side of the Newstead Road overbridge. 'Clara Cottages' were not casualties of war, but were replaced by more modern bungalows. The house on the left still stands...

...seen here in 2004.

No-one who was living or holidaying in Weymouth on 18 July 1955 will ever forget the torrential rain which fell overnight. At Martinstown 11" was recorded in a twenty-four-hour period, a UK record which still stands today. The swollen River Wey flooded all the villages along its route, and by the time the waters reached Westham Bridge they were carrying with them a huge mass of reeds torn from Radipole Lake. There was nowhere for this torrent to go except the town's streets and soon large areas were under water. Everyone looks remarkably cheerful, despite their flooded homes, as policemen row a most unusual 'milk float' down nearby Marsh Road to deliver the daily pinta.

More smiles as Newstead Road residents are ferried from their homes in July, 1955. The bridge in the background carried the Weymouth and Portland Railway over the roadway, but it was demolished in 1987, more than twenty years after the last train passed across it.

NEWTON'S COVE

The approach road – Newton's Road – to the GWR's proposed new port in Newton's Cove was under construction when this photograph was taken and the bridge over it was not yet built. These preliminary works were completed in 1902, but the whole scheme proceeded no further and the railway company abandoned its plans for Newton's Cove in 1913.

In 2003 extensive reconstruction and landscaping works were carried out at Newton's Cove. The large building in the background is The Centre for Environment, Fisheries and Aquaculture Science (CEFAS) Fish Health Inspectorate.

Newton's Cove, a scene from the 1960s, with the Nothe Gardens in the background.

The Nothe Gardens around 1930. First laid out in the late 1880s, the gardens have always been informally landscaped with shrubs and trees, and on this exposed and unstable coastline have been subjected to some severe landslips over the years.

In 1924 the Alexandra Gardens Theatre replaced the Kursaal, a glass structure built in 1913 around the gardens' Victorian outdoor bandstand. The redundant bandstand was then moved to the Nothe Gardens, where it can be seen in this view dating from 1925 or thereabouts. Such a shame that these pretty outdoor concert venues lost popularity. The bandstand, dating from 1891, was over seventy years old when it was removed from the Nothe site in 1964.

NORTH QUAY

This engraving, made from a drawing by H. Warren in the 1830s, was not published locally. Had it been, an error in the picture would surely have been noticed! The scene, entitled 'Weymouth', appears to depict the view along North Quay, from the artist's position somewhere at the foot of Boot Hill. The Town Bridge is shown – with Holy Trinity Church on the wrong side of the harbour! A likely explanation of this mistake is that the original painting was made before the church was built in 1836. In an attempt to update the subsequent mass-produced engraving, the church has been added – in the wrong place.

North Quay and Holy Trinity Church in 2004.

An early 1900s North Quay view shows the Hospital Parade, forerunner of today's Weymouth Carnival.

NOTHE FORT

This illustration from the early years of the nineteenth century shows the Nothe headland some fifty years before work commenced on building the Nothe Fort. On the headland stands a 'camera obscura' where Georgian visitors could enjoy a panoramic view of the resort, all done with mirrors. Tied up at the quayside is King George III's floating bathing machine, disused since 1805 when the King last holidayed in the resort. An ingenious design, the machine had underwater grills which allowed sea water to enter below deck, thus providing royal bathers with some privacy as they enjoyed a health-giving dip. Dressing rooms occupied the structure above the waterline. No-one knows what happened to the floating bathing machine – in all probability it ended up on dry land as a shed or store, which was also the fate of many wheeled bathing machines.

The prominent headland has long been utilised for the defence of Weymouth and Portland and this engraving of 1803 shows a modest gun emplacement on the Nothe.

In the 1840s the threat of an invasion by the French was a very great concern and the construction of major defence works began. The first breakwaters – two massive arms extending out from Portland – were built between 1849 and 1872. Complete with their own fortifications, they provided a safe naval anchorage in Portland Roads. Amongst the associated works were the Verne Citadel at Portland, and the great Nothe Fort, shown here under construction.

A Will Pye etching of the Nothe Fort.

The Nothe Fort was manned in both World Wars and continued to be used by the military until 1956, when the coastal artillery batteries were stood down. It then fell into disuse and became the haunt of vagrants who hastened the decay and dilapidation of its interior.

Fishing from the Stone Pier is a popular pastime and this 1960s' view looks back towards the massive fort.

In the 1970s the Nothe Fort was transformed, initially by a dedicated team of volunteers from Weymouth Civic Society, who laboured long and hard to bring the building back to life. Today the Fort is one of Weymouth's star tourist attractions, filled with superbly presented military history and providing unequalled views of the coast from its ramparts.

OSMINGTON VILLAGE

Where the A353 takes a sharp bend at Osmington on its way eastwards stands East Farm, seen here when traffic moved at a more leisurely pace along the main road.

Slightly more concealed by tree growth, the thatched building of East Farm is little changed today.

In what was once known as Post Office Lane and now as Village Street, the two properties in the foreground of this 1920s' photograph – Mr Tizard, the blind basket-maker's shop and the Post Office – have since been demolished. The postbox has been re-sited on a cottage wall in Chapel Lane.

In the centre of this 2004 photograph the cottage in the earlier view can be identified by its low thatched roofline. The demolished properties were originally replaced by two cottages, but these have since been converted into one residence – Wessex Cottage.

The cottage on the right-hand side of this photograph was one of the pair which replaced earlier buildings on this corner of Village Street and Church Lane.

On the right in 2004 is Wessex Cottage, the conversion of the two cottages into one house. At the corner of West Farm Lane and Church Lane is the 'Beehive', considerably extended since the earlier photograph.

OSMINGTON MILLS

The A353 separates Osmington village from Osmington Mills, which is reached by a long winding road leading to the coast. John Upham's set of eighteen engravings published in 1825 included 'Osmington Fall'. Gradual cliff erosion and flooding which followed the record downpour of July 1955 have since lowered the height of the Fall, sometimes called the Osmington Cascade.

The picturesque old Smugglers Inn at Osmington Mills dates back centuries – it was once the Picnic Inn and, before that, the Crown Inn. As can be seen here, the pub formerly occupied one tiny cottage.

Over the years, the 'Picnic' expanded into adjoining properties.

And in this photograph of the 1920s lobster teas and lunches were so popular that the 'Picnic Tea Rooms' was set up to cope with the demand.

The 'Picnic' was to become 'The Smugglers', appropriately, for in times past the inhabitants of Osmington Mills, in common with those in most other Dorset coastal villages, would tell their children to 'Watch the wall, my darling, while the Gentlemen go by' as the smugglers brought ashore 'Brandy for the Parson and Baccy for the Clerk'.

PARADES

Weymouth Esplanade provides a superb setting for military parades, such as this one in June 1998. The annual march-past of Veterans and ex-Servicemen takes place during the Military Festival each year with that in June 2004 taking on a special significance – the 60th anniversary of the D-Day landings.

In 1947, Major General Clayton L. Bissell, DSC, DFC, the US Military and Air Attaché, unveiled the American Memorial on the Esplanade, commemorating the half-million American troops who embarked on landing craft in Weymouth and Portland harbours prior to the Channel crossing which took them to fight on the Normandy beaches on D-Day, 6 June 1944. On that historic day on the French shore, over three thousand men lost their lives or were wounded on Omaha Beach alone.

'Bravo Dorsets' reads the banner stretched across King Street as men of the Dorset Regiment return home from South Africa in 1902, at the end of the Boer War.

The focal point for the GIs remembering their fallen comrades at the 2004 commemorations. In recent years plaques have been added to the monument recalling other American losses, in particular the sinking by the enemy of the troopship *SS Leopoldville* in the English Channel on Christmas Day 1944, with the loss of some 800 lives.

There was a huge turnout in May 1914 when Admiral Lord Charles Beresford was granted the Freedom of the Borough. The Admiral had been Commander-in-Chief of the Channel Fleet at Portland from 1907 – 1909.

A second striking scene on the
Esplanade in May 1914.

THE PIER

Artist William Daniell toured the coast of England in the early 1800s, recording port and harbour scenes. This is his view of Weymouth in 1823. He published his aquatints (more than 300) as part-works in a series entitled *A Voyage round Great Britain*.

An engraving of the 1830s shows a cross-channel paddle steamer leaving the port in the days when the pier hardly extended seaward beyond the round house in Devonshire Buildings.

In the 1840s and 1850s the pier was considerably extended and the shape of the resulting structure was to remain largely unchanged, apart from the addition of passenger and baggage handling facilities, until the early 1930s.

These Victorian engravings, often sold as sets bound into little books of 6 or 12 illustrations, were popular holiday souvenirs.

The pier has welcomed many important visitors over the years and here Mayor Bartle Pye greets King George V on 11 May 1912.

The main purpose of the King's visit in 1912 was to review the naval fleet. It was to be an historic occasion, as for the first time ever a plane took off from the deck of a moving warship, HMS *Hibernia*. The pilot was Lieutenant Charles Samson.

Weymouth's lifeboat *Friern Watch* (the second to bear this name) was standing-by in 1912 as the Royal Yacht *Victoria and Albert* took King George V out into the Channel to watch exercises by the Royal Navy's Home and Atlantic Fleets.

Pier facilities proved inadequate for twentieth-century harbour trade and work on a massive reconstruction began early in 1931. It was declared complete in 1933 and formally opened by the Prince of Wales (later King Edward VIII). The scale of the rebuilding can be seen in this photograph from 1932.

Dockers unload potatoes from the Channel Islands in this 1930s' view of the newly extended pier.

A superb aerial photograph of the 1933 pier. It was taken in August 1939, just a month before war broke out. A detailed study of this picture reveals the layout of the streets of Chapelhay, which were soon to be subjected to repeated air raids.

Yet more pier extensions and alterations in the 1970s (when the car ferry terminal opened) and 1980s (when the extension shown here was finished) completely changed its shape to that which we still see today.

The Channel Islands boat train was once a familiar sight, wending its way through Weymouth's streets taking its passengers to and from Weymouth Railway Station and the Pier. Seen here about to cross King Street, the train is hauled by a pannier tank engine in the days before diesels took over the service. Note, just forward of the cab, the bell carried to warn pedestrians of the train's approach.

And onto the vast reclaimed pier area shown opposite were offloaded hundreds of new cars imported from the France and Spain in the early 1980s. The cars shown here were waiting to be loaded onto transporters for onward delivery by road.

PORTLAND HARBOUR

A busy scene showing Portland Harbour during the construction of Portland Breakwaters is perhaps more interesting for its depiction of Portland Railway Station. The Weymouth and Portland Railway had opened in 1865 – this little engraving was probably produced that year.

This view shows Isambard Kingdom Brunel's *Great Eastern* at Portland in the late 1860s. This was not her first visit for in 1859 the ship had spent several weeks in the harbour undergoing extensive repairs following a serious explosion on board during her acceptance trials. *The Great Eastern* was never a commercial success and in the 1860s she was converted for transatlantic cable laying. At Portland preparation for these voyages were supervised by Daniel Gooch, Brunel's successor at the GWR. Gooch was a frequent visitor to the local area during these years and he later returned for holidays. Spending Xmas 1881 in Weymouth, he recorded in his diary on 27 December 'We walked to Wyke Regis this morning and back by way of Rodwell. This latter place is growing very fast. The views are beautiful, looking over Portland and the bay. Day fine.' And on the 28th 'This has been a lovely day. Before lunch we went to the pier and sat there in bright sunshine, the water in the bay being as smooth as glass, more like a summer day...'

Another famous ship was a visitor to Portland in 1976 – the Royal Yacht *Britannia*. No longer in royal service, she will not be seen here again, as since de-commissioning in 1997 the yacht has moved to a permanent berth at Leith in Scotland.

The focus of this 1950 photograph is not shipping, but the units seen in the background of the picture which was taken during the construction of Q Pier at Portland. They played an important part in the nation's history. These are the concrete Phoenix Units which were taken across the Channel on D-Day, 6 June 1944 to become part of the temporary Mulberry Harbours used for landing troops, transport and supplies on the beaches of Normandy. In 1953 a number of those shown in this photograph were taken to Holland to help repair damage caused by devastating floods. Just two Phoenix Units remain in Portland Harbour today and they are the only ones in Britain. Due to their historic role in World War II they are now preserved as Listed Buildings.

PORTWEY HOSPITAL

Portwey Hospital is remembered primarily as the town's Maternity Hospital, many locals having been born there between 1948 and 1987. It was originally built in 1836 as the Poor Law Union Workhouse and remained as such until the early 1930s when the responsibility for poor relief was taken over by the local authorities. The Union Workhouse records would have been of great interest, but unfortunately few survive, the majority having been disposed of during a World War II salvage drive. Portwey's transition to a maternity hospital came after its service as a wartime emergency hospital.

After Portwey Maternity Hospital's closure in 1987, the buildings lay empty for some years but they have now been converted to housing, and today the original exceptionally long frontage on Wyke Road looks much as it did in the nineteenth century.

PRESTON BEACH ROAD

This rather bleak view of Greenhill dates from the 1880s.

Not all of the houses which face the beach at Greenhill were completed when this postcard was published. It probably dates from around 1900 and was produced in Germany, as were many early picture postcards. Bathing machines this far along the beach are an unusual feature – most were down on the sands and available for hire, but these may have been privately owned.

'Sugar-em Shorey' was one of the great characters of Weymouth. He, and his father before him, inhabited this little building on Preston Beach Road, a former tollhouse. The family ran a horse-and-carriage hire business and Sugar-em later went into the log trade. The old tollhouse lacked all modern amenities such as running water and electricity, and in the 1950s the Shoreys (Sugar-em and his sister) moved reluctantly into council accommodation and their old home was demolished.

The photographer's intention in the previous photograph was not to illustrate the Shoreys' billboard-flanked house, but was to record one of the many occasions when rough seas dumped hundreds of tons of shingle on the Preston Beach Road. It rather looks as though this optimistic motorist attempting to dig his car out of the pebbles was more likely to be swept off his feet as another wave crashed over the old sea wall.

The height of the old wall can clearly be seen in another shingle-strewn view of Preston Beach Road.

This Southern National double decker bus received a fair wallop from the grab of a crane being used in shingle clearing operations in 1962. Fortunately there were no passengers on the front seats of the upper deck when the accident happened.

Behind the Preston Beach Wall lies Lodmoor, seen here in the 1950s when there was no planned nature reserve on the marshy ground and houses were just starting to appear on the higher land.

Another 1950s view shows the service station, forerunner of a larger garage on the site which has now been replaced by 'The Front', a skateboard facility.

Since 1995 a new sea defence wall and promenade have linked Overcombe Corner with Greenhill and road closures on stormy days are a thing of the past.

In the 1920s this petrol station stood on Overcombe Corner. The building was later replaced, but the garage eventually closed. The row of coastguard cottages in the background was intact then, but erosion of the cliffs here saw several of them slip down to the shore before coastal protection works were carried out in the 1970s– saving two of them.

Houses and a public convenience built in the early years of the twenty-first century now fill the site of the garage.

PRESTON VILLAGE

On the main Preston Road in the 1920s stood Pratt's Garage, William Tawse the family butcher and a B&B offering teas and refreshments.

In 2004 the garage has gone, but the shop and house, although much altered, remain. This is now the Co-op's convenience store.

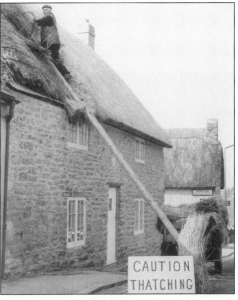

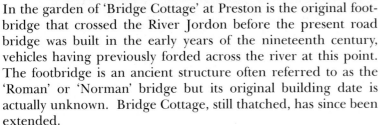

In the garden of 'Bridge Cottage' at Preston is the original footbridge that crossed the River Jordon before the present road bridge was built in the early years of the nineteenth century, vehicles having previously forded across the river at this point. The footbridge is an ancient structure often referred to as the 'Roman' or 'Norman' bridge but its original building date is actually unknown. Bridge Cottage, still thatched, has since been extended.

The skilled and ancient craft of the thatcher was on display on the main road at Preston in the latter half of the twentieth century. The former Post Office building is in the background, the PO having now relocated to the opposite side of Preston Road.

This 1910 view shows the road through Preston as it heads towards White Horse Hill. Not only are the traffic levels dramatically higher today, but the road itself is very much wider.

PUNCH AND JUDY

The seaside was not the birthplace of Punch and Judy: the outdoor puppet theatre had its origins in seventeenth century Italy. Generations of children have enjoyed the penetrating nasal voices and traditional knockabout violence of the puppet characters, whose stripy booth was a familiar sight on the sands in the 1920s...

... and still is today. The current Weymouth puppeteer is Professor Guy Higgins, who has put on his twice daily summer shows in the season since 1975. His long serving predecessor was Frank Edmonds.

QUEEN VICTORIA STATUE

This procession making its way along King Street in 1902 was conveying Princess Henry of Battenberg, the youngest daughter of Queen Victoria, to Greenhill where she was to unveil a statue of the late Queen. In earlier years the adjacent Queen Street, until it was renamed, was known as King Street West. The Fountain Hotel was still in business then and the spire in the background is that of Christ Church, a relatively new building in 1902, having been consecrated in 1874. Diminishing congregations in the early 1930s led to the church building being declared redundant, although it was not actually demolished until 1956.

The very busy King Street today, with traffic filtering down off The Esplanade. The main change, apart from the modes of transport, is the absence of Christ Church.

The site chosen for Queen Victoria's statue was this spot in front of St John's Church, an area previously occupied by an ornate lamp standard and a fountain. The photograph dates from the 1880s.

The statue of Queen Victoria a postcard view from the early 1900s.

RADIPOLE

The imposing grey stone 'Abbots Court' once stood in extensive grounds at the northern end of Radipole Lake, which was an isolated spot before the roads with 'Lake District' names were laid out at Radipole. The mansion was built in 1895 by John Bagg, local builder and three times Mayor of Weymouth in the early 1900s. Bagg over-reached himself both in business and lifestyle, and he was declared bankrupt in 1910. In the 1920s the house was owned by Thomas Burberry, whose company today is still famed for its classic trenchcoat design and range of 'Burberry check' accessories.

John Bagg's house was demolished in 1987 and these flats, built on its site, now overlook the lake. They have retained the name of Abbots Court.

By the early years of the twentieth century the development of the Ullswater Crescent area (then known as Abbots Court Road) had begun. John Bagg's house is on the left. There was no road along the eastern shore of Radipole Lake, and the infilling on which Radipole Park Drive was to be built was not commenced until the 1920s. The chimney on the right-hand side of the photograph probably belonged to a small brickworks, one of many such then in production around the town.

A November 1977 view from Skew Bridge on Dorchester Road shows a derelict Mount Pleasant Farmhouse.

Tree growth in the area has completely obscured the same view today, where the Safeway Supermarket opened on the site of the old farm in 1991. Extensive commercial development by the New Look company of the area beyond the railway led to the building of a new approach road – Mercery Road – where this stone bearing the company's logo stands on the corner. In 2004 New Look announced plans to move its distribution centre elsewhere in the UK, with inevitable job losses in the local area.

This view from the 1790s is of another farm in the Radipole area. The engraving is described as 'View taken from behind Redlands Farm House about 6 miles from Dorchester'. John Hutchins' *History and Antiquities of the County of Dorset* provides the alternative name 'Knacker's Hole' for the Redlands area.

A fine photograph from around 1910 takes us down Radipole Lane to its junction with Causeway.

The scene is not greatly changed today, although once again, almost a century's tree growth obscures much of the old view.

At the bottom of the hill, the bridge which crosses the River Wey was damaged in the severe floods of 1955, and the residents in the cottage in the centre of the picture were rescued by boat. The cottages on the left have since been demolished.

Radipole's ancient church of St Ann and the neighbouring Manor House: a painting of 1816 by John Upham.

Upham also made this sketch of the church in 1827, showing the building's unusual bell cote, with provision for three bells. The church has its origins in the thirteenth century.

This picturesque view of Radipole and its church appeared in John Love's collection of engravings published in 1790. The views were by different artists this one was drawn by A Beaumont and engraved by James Fittler. Love dedicated the work to HRH The Duke of Gloucester, whose house Gloucester Lodge, on the Esplanade, became the holiday home of King George III.

Radipole's second C of E church, St Aldhelm's, dates from the late 1940s although its façade is much altered today.

RAILWAY STATION

Countless thousands of passengers passed through the Brunel-designed, wooden roofed railway station (centre) between 1857, when the service to Weymouth commenced, and 1986 when the old buildings were replaced. This is the only known early photograph of the station, taken by noted local photographer William Thompson. The terminus was described at the time as being 'extensive, but with no architectural pretensions'.

Weymouth Station has seen many royal visitors over the years. Here King Edward VIII prepares to depart in November 1936, following a visit to the Channel Fleet – one of his last official duties before the Abdication.

Edward VIII had also visited Weymouth several times as Prince of Wales. Here he is arriving at Weymouth Railway Station in 1923 where the royal train was waiting to take him back to London following a visit to Duchy of Cornwall lands in the area.

By 1984, as we can see here, the original station had fallen into disrepair...

...and in the spring of 1986 demolition crews began dismantling the station buildings which had served the town for more than 120 years.

The present railway station opened in October, 1986. Set further back from King Street than the old Brunel buildings, it is of a modern and purely functional design.

In December 1949 Mayor Alfred Burt had the honour of naming British Railway's West Country class locomotive 34091 *Weymouth* after the town.

Probably one of the most striking contrasts – then (1959) Weymouth Engine Sheds, with coal wagons in profusion…

…and now (2004). The former railway property has since been covered by the houses of Milton Crescent, Milton Close, Princes Drive, Lindens Close and Southfield Avenue.

RIDGEWAY

Another of John Upham's '1825' series of prints shows the then newly-opened road (now the A354) that took traffic up Ridgeway Hill. It was intended to provide an alternative to the steep gradients of the old Roman Road over Gould's Hill at Upwey, although the new road's sharp hairpin bend had to be negotiated with care. The raw chalk face of the recent excavations can be clearly seen in Upham's view.

The road has been considerably widened in the intervening 180 years, but this is the view taken from approximately the same spot in 2004.

ROYAL YARD

Royal Yard takes its name from its situation and use. It stands at the rear of Gloucester Lodge, the holiday home of King George III from 1789 – 1805, and it was the site of the royal stables. A cinema opened here in 1933 and the building incorporated some of the structure of the former royal property (right).

Royal Yard in 2004, some 100 years after the previous photograph was taken. Temporary buildings on the left herald the arrival of builders to work on the site of the cinema, which closed at the end of October 1999.

The cinema had opened in 1933 as the Odeon and it underwent several name changes in its lifetime, becoming the Classic, Cannon and Picturedrome before finally closing. Its original name, Odeon, stood for Oscar Deutsch Entertains Our Nation – Deutsch being the owner of the cinema chain. The site will now be used for housing, within which will be incorporated a surviving fragment of the original Georgian structure.

SHOPS

Talbot the Draper occupied Albion House, on the corner of St Mary Street and St Alban Street. The bold lettering above the first floor can still be seen today.

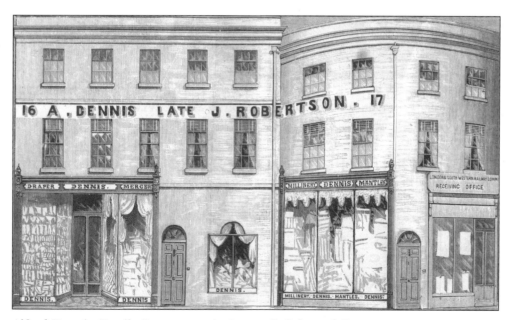

Alfred Dennis, Family Draper, was in Lower St Edmund Street.

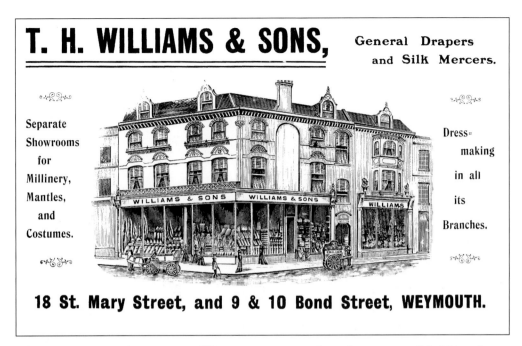

Another draper's shop, T H Williams & Sons, stood on the corner of St Mary Street and Bond Street...

...completely rebuilt, this is currently the HSBC Bank, seen here in its Midland Bank days.

Gosdens the Grocer, located at 45 St Mary Street, was a supplier to the military.

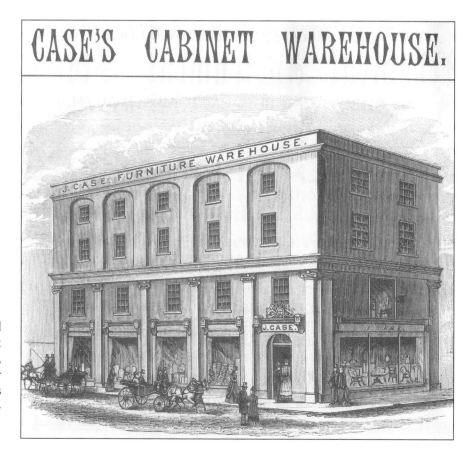

Case's Cabinet Warehouse still stands on the corner of St Mary Street and Bond Street, now occupied by shoe retailer tReds. It was for many years Bennett and Escott's premises, electricians.

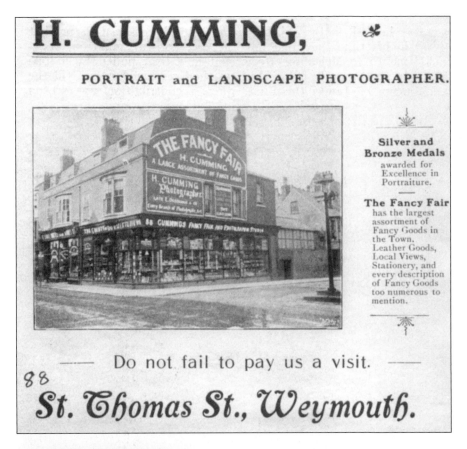

H. CUMMING,

PORTRAIT and LANDSCAPE PHOTOGRAPHER.

Silver and Bronze Medals awarded for Excellence in Portraiture.

The Fancy Fair has the largest assortment of Fancy Goods in the Town. Leather Goods, Local Views, Stationery, and every description of Fancy Goods too numerous to mention.

—— Do not fail to pay us a visit. ——

88
St. Thomas St., Weymouth.

Cumming the photographer's 'Fancy Fair' was on the corner of St Thomas Street and School Street...

...where the upper wall has long been used as advertising space, as seen here in the days of occupancy by Whittles. Today the advert directs shoppers to the nearby Colwell Centre.

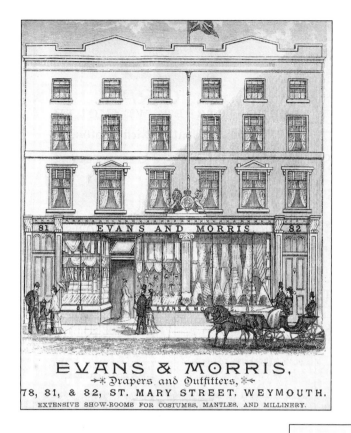

EVANS & MORRIS,
Drapers and Outfitters,
78, 81, & 82, ST. MARY STREET, WEYMOUTH.
EXTENSIVE SHOW-ROOMS FOR COSTUMES, MANTLES, AND MILLINERY.

Another draper – Evans and Morris – is now Boots the Chemist, which still has the same very recognisable façade above, but with the ubiquitous twentieth century plate glass at street level. Boots' predecessor in this St Mary Street shop was the hardware store Timothy Whites and Taylors.

In the early 1900s Andrew Graham's Phoenix Aerated Water Factory was in St Nicholas Street and the company's embossed green glass bottles still turn up today. The same company owned Graham's Bar in New Street, scene of a much publicised murder in 1902 when a young barmaid, Hettie Stephens, was shot dead there by Edward Simmons, a steward at the nearby Royal Dorset Yacht Club. His motive was unclear – he had struck up a friendship with Hettie and given her gifts, but apparently to her it had not seemed to be a serious relationship. Simmons, a married man, did not deny the shooting, but was judged to be insane at his trial and was sent to Broadmoor.

SIDNEY HALL

In the latter half of the twentieth century the Sidney Hall, located at the foot of Boot Hill, was used for roller-skating and then bingo. It is seen here shortly before its demolition in 1987. The Hall had opened in 1900 and was built by Sir John Groves, head of the local brewing firm, as a memorial to his son Sidney, who died in the 1890s.

In its eighty+ years, lifetime, the Sidney Hall was put to many uses. Built originally as a meeting place for the Church Lads Brigade, it later became a World War I hospital; a temporary school for children bombed out of their own school buildings in World War II; a venue for exhibitions and shows; a roller skating rink; a bingo hall – and there are probably more! Today nothing remains of the Sidney Hall and its companion the Small Sidney Hall – where they stood, shoppers now park their cars in front of the Asda supermarket. Armed with money off vouchers from the store they once could have obtained their motor fuel from...

...Broadwey Motors petrol station in Marsh Road. Above the forecourt, on Boot Hill, were the premises of the Weymouth & Portland Snooker Club but both are now gone, replaced in the early years of this century by the apartment block known as Spinnaker View.

Many of the town's larger buildings and some sizeable private houses were pressed into use as hospitals during the First World War to cope with increasing numbers of casualties returning from the fighting in Europe. This is the interior of the Sidney Hall, converted to hospital use.

The town saw many wounded Australian troops from 1915 onwards – the sites of their camps and convalescent centres are commemorated in Australian road and street names in Chickerell, Westham and Littlemoor. Those who died here are buried in the Newstead Road cemetery; their graves lie next to the Cross of Remembrance erected by the Commonwealth War Graves Commission.

SPRING GARDENS

The houses shown here in Spring Gardens no longer exist. They formed an attractive terrace linking Rodwell Avenue and St Leonard's Road and had long front gardens. The railings in the bottom left-hand corner of this 1900s photograph still surround Hobart Cottages in Rodwell Avenue. Although much of Chapelhay was blitzed around it in World War II, Spring Gardens was not too badly damaged but it was cleared in post-war years as part of the complete redevelopment of the Chapelhay area.

The post-war Spring Gardens cannot be seen from the same vantage point today, but the railings of yesteryear are still very much in evidence.

Today's Spring Gardens is a cul-de-sac of red brick houses, off St Leonard's Road.

ST MARTIN'S CHURCH

The rapid late-nineteenth century development of the Pye Hill district along Chickerell Road led to the establishment of 'St Martin's Mission' for those living in this area of Holy Trinity Parish. In 1906 it was decided to erect a permanent church building for the growing congregation, and the foundation stone of St Martin's Church was laid on 30 October 1907. Here, clergy process from Holy Trinity Church to the site of the new church for the stone laying ceremony.

What had been intended as the first section of the church, the nave, is seen here under construction. In fact, this was all that was built; planned side aisles and other extensions were never added, hence the tall narrow shape of St Martin's.

The red brick interior of St Martin's; consecrated on 30 October 1908 as a chapel of ease to Holy Trinity Church.

The eventual closure of the church led to its conversion for residential use in the early 1980s, when the bell turret was removed. This photograph was taken in 2004 and the church is now known as St Martin's Court, Chickerell Road.

In post-World War II years St Martin's is probably best remembered as the church for the Deaf and Hard of Hearing, for whom it also provided club facilities. Later the building, which was refurbished in 1961 to provide both church and hall, became HQ for the Weymouth and Portland Branch of the Dorset Association for the Disabled.

SWANS

This appealing 1930s' photograph of the swans being fed just above Westham Bridge also has much of interest in its background scene. Radipole Park Drive was then a highway at this point, but the area today is totally pedestrianised. Beyond Melcombe Regis Gardens can be seen Betts and Company's timber sheds which stood on what is now Park Street Car Park. The New Bridge Hotel on the Commercial Road/Westham Road corner was demolished in 2003 and has been replaced by an apartment building.

Now that the whole area above Westham Bridge has been redeveloped, the swans tend to congregate on the opposite shore where they know that many pedestrians emerging from the underpass will be carrying a bagful of food for them. On the day that we visited the scene in the previous photograph just one swan was taking advantage of this small girl's offering.

TOWN BRIDGE

A 'Town Bridge' has crossed the harbour since 1597 when the inhabitants of the once separate towns of Weymouth and Melcombe Regis finally decided to put an end to centuries spent disputing harbour rights and to accept their enforced Union of 1571. Prior to this, the only means of crossing the water was by ferry-boat. Various bridges have come and gone since the sixteenth century and our present Town Bridge dates from 1930. Here, a small crowd watches demolition work on its predecessor in 1928. Reconstruction would also entail the removal of Town Bridge Buildings in the centre of the picture.

This view dates from the 1920s, when motor cars were beginning to take over from the horse-drawn carriage. Fascinating detail in the background shows (from the left) a harbour warehouse, Town Bridge Buildings, Strong & Williams shop at the bottom of St Thomas Street and the Palladium Cinema. A goods train makes its way along Custom House Quay.

An intrepid trio, which included Mayor Percy Boyle and Town Clerk Percy Smallman, is swung out in a bucket to view the cofferdam used in the construction of the new Town Bridge.

The new bridge, almost ready for opening. Temporary stands have been erected (bottom right) for guests to view the proceedings.

Opening day, 4 July 1930. The Duke of York, later King George VI, steps out across the bridge he has just declared open.

Looking down St Thomas Street in its pre-pedestrianised days, with the Southern National 273 bus heading for the Southlands Estate.

A Town Bridge scene from the 1960s. The brick built office block which replaced the Town Bridge Buildings seen in the earlier photographs, is a very obvious new feature and is of a typical 1950s' design. In the summer of 2004, stripped of its bland façade, the now skeletal structure awaits conversion to apartments.

UPWEY VILLAGE

Upwey Wishing Well developed from the health-giving 'Springs', which had been a tourist attraction for Georgian visitors to the resort. A late-nineteenth century writer, Hawley Smart, used Upwey as a setting and introduced the 'Wishing Well' name for the water source in his novel *Broken Bonds*, published in 1874. This picture dates from the early 1900s when there was a wooden shelter at the Well.

At Upwey, the parish church of St Laurence is little changed today. This is another of John Upham's '1825' engravings.

In 1923 the Prince of Wales, during his tour of Duchy of Cornwall property in the Weymouth and Dorchester area, sipped the well water and presumably followed the tradition of making a wish. Cameras are not supposed to lie, but it is obvious that the Prince's photograph has been superimposed on this postcard of Upwey Wishing Well, turning it into a special souvenir edition! The card also shows the stone shelter erected at the well in the early 1900s by the Gould family of Upwey, the initials G.T.I.G over the arch being those of George Thomas Ingleheim Gould.

It was once possible to alight from the train at Upwey Wishing Well Halt, although it was still a fair walk to the well in Church Street (note the olde-worlde 'Halte' on the station's name board, a spelling favoured by the GWR at that time). The little station opened in 1905 and lasted just over fifty years, closing in January 1957. It was adjacent to the present road bridge, which takes the railway over the Dorchester Road. Steps, which still exist, led down from both platforms to street level. It was the third station to include Upwey in its name, Upwey Junction (later Upwey and Broadwey) being on the main line, and Upwey serving the Abbotsbury branch.

Upwey's Church Street retains the charm of an earlier age. This view, of around 1905, is easily recognisable today, and the row of cottages on the right hand side is little changed apart from tiles which have replaced roof thatch.

Once again in Church Street, these are the thatched cottages visible in the background on the previous photograph. The view is slightly later date, probably around 1925, and shows 'Windsbatch' and 'Wishing Well' cottages both originally built in the eighteenth century. Beyond can be seen the old Rectory, now known as Batchfoot House.

VICTORIA HOTEL

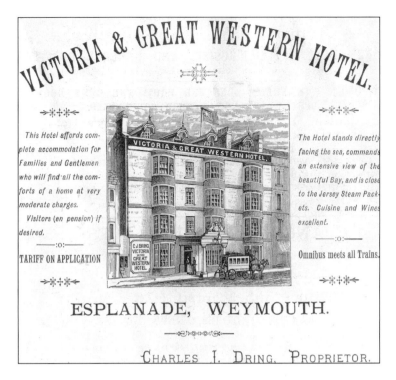

'The Vic' on the Esplanade was formerly the 'Victoria and Great Western Hotel'. In this 1880s' advertisement the proprietor was Charles Dring, but in earlier years the Luce family ran the establishment, followed by the Scrivens, when it was known as Scrivens Boarding House. Above the hotel doorway in this drawing is what appears to be the royal coat-of-arms, which was later replaced by a sculpted bust of Queen Victoria.

The Victoria underwent a name change in the twentieth century, becoming the 'Fairhaven', part of the King family's hotel chain, and following recent refurbishment is now known as 'The New Vic'.

WEYMOUTH COLLEGE

Weymouth College, on Dorchester Road, was a boys' public school from the 1860s until 1940. A long list of distinguished Old Boys includes air ace George Stainforth, author John Meade Falkner, broadcaster Stuart Hibberd, and Henry Sturmey, of Sturmey-Archer bicycle fame. Shortly after the outbreak of World War II, all the boys transferred to Wellingborough, Northants and the school did not return. After early wartime use as a de-gaussing centre, and then a temporary hospital when the nearby Weymouth and District Hospital was bombed, the buildings were used in post war years as a Teacher Training College and a College of Higher Education before the present Weymouth College (a tertiary college) took over the site in 1985.

WEYMOUTH COLLEGE.

A PUBLIC SCHOOL EDUCATION (Classical and Modern) AT A MODERATE COST.

HEAD MASTER ... ... REV. JOHN MILLER, B.D.
SECOND MASTER ... ... REV. F. T. HARRISON, B.A.
THIRD MASTER ... ... T. B. WAITT, ESQ., B.A.
With Seven Assistant Masters.

FEES.

For Board, Tuition, Stationery, and Laundress.—£21 a Term for Boys under 11 years ; £24 for Boys under 13 years ; £30 for Sandhurst and Woolwich Pupils.
DAY BOYS.—Fees for Tuition and Stationery.—Five Guineas for Boys under 11 years ; Six Guineas for Boys under 13 years.

Weymouth College now occupies new buildings on grounds off Cranford Avenue, behind the old public school. The redundant Victorian college and its adjacent chapel still stand, very successfully converted to apartments.

Almost unnoticed in the old College grounds stands a remnant of Radipole Farm, which once occupied some 600 acres of land on both sides of Dorchester Road. When the farm was put up for sale in 1802, a plan showed what is now known as 'Radipole Farmhouse' or 'Nangles Farm' as the 'New House', with an older farmhouse standing further north, on the opposite side of the road. It is the 'New House' which is shown here, and it, too, has been restored by the developers of the old Weymouth College site. Much of the land north of St John's Church eventually came into the possession of the Johnstone Estate, owners of extensive property in the town. Henry Nangle was agent to Sir Frederic Johnstone and the alternative name 'Nangle's Farm' probably has some connection with this ownership of the land.

Weymouth College, the boys' public school, began life in this familiar building (now the Arts Centre), which today is one of the few survivors of extensive redevelopment along Commercial Road.

WEYMOUTH GRAMMAR SCHOOL

Weymouth Grammar School was founded in Westham's Alma Road in 1913 as the Victoria Secondary Schools, changing its name to Weymouth Secondary School before becoming Weymouth Grammar School in 1927. An additional 'New Wing' and a collection of huts housed its students until the 1960s, when the school moved out to Charlestown, eventually becoming Budmouth Technology College. The South Dorset Technical College (later Weymouth College) took over the buildings and land but sold them to developers when all the college departments transferred to the present Cranford Avenue site. In this 1980s view, the former Grammar School buildings are the two on the left hand side of the picture, that in the centre is a College building of the 1970s, with the original South Dorset Technical College of 1939 on the far right.

Today all trace of the educational establishments has gone and the houses of 'College Heights'...

...now fill the site alongside Weymouth Way (the road built to link Westham with Dorchester Road in the 1980s). Pottery Lane, which led to the College took its name from old Weymouth Brick Tile and Pottery Works, which operated on the site from the 1860s until the early years of the twentieth century. The new houses commemorate this link, having roads named after rather more famous English pottery companies, such as Wedgwood, Goss, Aynsley and Doulton.

Westham itself saw very little housing development until the last quarter of the nineteenth century, when the town, with a growing population and a shortage of building land, turned its sights to the fields across the Backwater. This was the first 'Westham Bridge', a timber structure of the 1850s, which was replaced by the present Westham Bridge in 1921. The view looks from the Melcombe Regis side towards a very empty Westham shore.

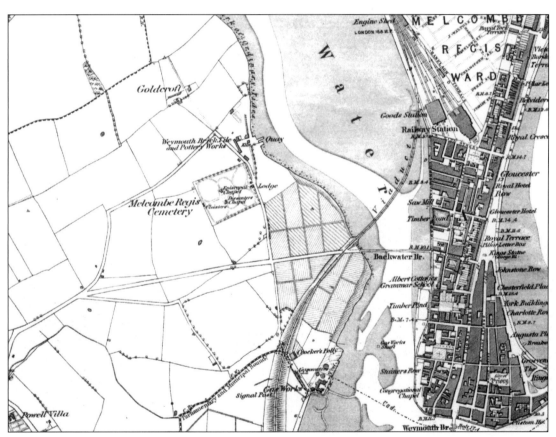

This map, drawn in 1864, shows that for some residents their journey across the old Westham Bridge may well have been the last one they were to make, as, apart from the Brickworks and the isolated Goldcroft Farm, there was little at Westham apart from the cemetery. The Grammar School and College sites later occupied land between the pottery works and the railway crossing.

Three Westham scenes from the twentieth century, all with a transport theme. In this photograph the Abbotsbury Road level crossing gates are closed for a train on the Weymouth and Portland Railway. This was Littlefield Crossing, and Westham Halt opened nearby in 1909. Flats now occupy land in front of the church (left) and the site of the now-demolished Health Centre (right).

A train of rather smaller scale takes its passengers under the steel girder bridge which carried the Weymouth and Portland Railway across Radipole Lake. The bridge was demolished in the 1970s, the railway having closed to passengers in 1952 and to goods in 1965. A clear view up the Lake was enjoyed for a few years before the Swannery Road Bridge was constructed in the late 1980s, conveying vehicles across the water more or less where the old rail bridge stood.

The miniature train in the previous picture was heading for the terminus, shown here, on Westham Car Park. This area was completely altered in the 1980s by the construction of the relief road scheme. Both the miniature railway scenes probably date from the 1950s.

WEYMOUTH HYDRO

Weymouth Hydro offered 'holidays and health' from the 1950s–1970s at 31 Greenhill. Therapies on offer included tonic treatments, osteopathy, naturopathy and massage, plus foam and pine baths and health-giving food. In its later years the building was converted to become The White House residential home.

After the home's closure, the former Hydro was pulled down and this development – 'Waves' apartments – replaced it early in the twenty-first century.

WORLD WAR II

As war threatened, 1939 saw local residents turning up at appointed collection centres to be issued with gas masks, the horrific effects of mustard gas attacks on men in the trenches of World War I being well remembered. This demonstration was held at the council depot, then on Westwey Road.

Chapelhay was to bear the brunt of air attacks on Weymouth during World War II, with whole streets being devastated and many lives lost. This post-war scene of an overgrown site at the top of Chapelhay Steps was formerly where Holy Trinity School stood – it was severely damaged in a 1940 air raid and pulled down after the war. Trinity Court, homes for the elderly, has since been built here. This had been an unlucky spot in time of war for the mediaeval chapel which gave its name to Chapelhay also stood here but was so badly damaged during seventeenth-century Civil War fighting that it, too, had been demolished in an earlier age.

Weymouth, for a town of its size, was one of the most heavily bombed in the country. In 1941 the home of the wartime mayor was badly damaged in an air raid. Joe Goddard Mayor and publican of the 'Royal Adelaide' on Abbotsbury Road was retrieved injured, fortunately not too seriously, from the wreckage, above which a Union Jack has been hoisted. The raid occurred in November, shortly before the mayoral election was held, and Mayor Goddard was taken from the nursing home where he was recuperating to be sworn in as Mayor once more – a popular man who held the office throughout the war years.

A number of enemy planes were downed in the local area. Here Doug Acutt stands alongside the wing of one which crashed near the Civil Defence depot in Cranford Avenue. Remembered by many locals as a teacher at Melcombe Regis School, Doug Acutt was also a St John Ambulance Brigade member and Civil Defence volunteer – who in 1945 published *Brigade in Action: The History of the Origin and Development of the St John Ambulance Brigade in Weymouth and of its Co-operation with the Civil Defence Services during the war 1939 to 1945*, an invaluable record of wartime Weymouth.

Just one enemy plane was responsible for the destruction of the Southern National bus garage in Edward Street and damage to many houses in the vicinity when it dropped three high explosive bombs on 21 October 1940. Three men and two children died in the raid.

The tide of war turned when the vast D-Day invasion force landed on the beaches of northern France on D-Day, 6 June 1944. In the months beforehand, the Americans were here in force, and preparations for the invasion were secret and intense before wave after wave of US troops would make their way down Weymouth seafront to embark on landing craft in Weymouth and Portland harbours for the Channel crossing and their destination – Omaha Beach – from which many would not return. This photograph of American troops en route for the quayside is one of the best-known of the local wartime pictures.

WYKE REGIS

An 1880s' view taken from Foord's Corner at Wyke Regis looks across empty fields, with the road to Portland almost bereft of buildings. The housing developments in 'new' Wyke would begin a decade later when Robert Whitehead set up his torpedo factory at Ferrybridge. Homes for his workers followed as houses were built along and in the streets leading off Portland Road.

Today almost all the green fields have gone, much more of the open space having been filled in the early 1950s with the houses of the Downclose Estate.

Victoria Road was one of the 'Whitehead' streets. Local school facilities proved inadequate for the children of the factory's growing workforce, so Robert Whitehead funded the building of a new school at the end of Victoria Road in 1897. It was replaced by the present school in 1985.

The scene in Victoria Road today.

Cows meander up Portland Road towards All Saints' Church in this early twentieth century scene. The cottages on the right hand side are just past Portland Road's junction with Chamberlaine Road. The house in the centre has been demolished.

This photograph is a little difficult to identify, but the buildings are thought to be those of the 'Old Home Farm' at Wyke Regis. The angle from which it is taken makes All Saints Road, off Wyke Square, appear less steep than it is today, but early maps do show buildings of this shape and size along the west side of the street.

The farm was demolished in the 1890s, when this family group photograph was taken beside the farmhouse.

The scene today.

Wyke Castle stands at the junction of Westhill Road and Pirates Lane. It was never a fortification, merely an architectural whim built in the mid-nineteenth century at the behest of a wealthy and perhaps slightly eccentric Victorian gentleman.

Today the Castle, a little altered, provides three separate dwellings.

In Wyke churchyard lie generations of Wyke residents. Local artist John William Upham's pictures have appeared throughout this book and it is fitting that we should end with his 1825 engraving of All Saints' Church. John Upham died in 1828 and he is buried here, close to the church which was the subject of several of his paintings.